Spiritual Longing in a Woman's World

Lisa Lewton

Copyright ©2021 by Lisa Lewton

Edited by Naomi Thorson

All rights reserved. No part of this book may be reproduced, stored in a retrieval system, or transmitted in any form or by any means, electronic or mechanical, including photocopying, recording, or otherwise, without prior written permission of the author, except in the case of brief quotations embodied in critical reviews and certain other noncommercial uses permitted by copyright law. Permission may be requested through author website: www.lisalewton.com.

Unless otherwise noted, the Scripture quotations are from New Revised Standard Version Bible, copyright ©1989 National Council of the Churches of Christ in the United States of America. Used by permission. All rights reserved worldwide.

ISBN: 978-0-578-91598-2

For Marcus, Tom, Sam, and Karis: the reason I have anything to write.

And for my first church, Our Savior Lutheran Church in Sherwood, North Dakota; my internship congregation, Oak Grove Lutheran Church in Richfield, Minnesota; my first call, Holy Nativity Lutheran Church in New Hope, Minnesota; and my current call, St. John Evangelical Lutheran Church in Dickinson, North Dakota. Thank you for welcoming me into the sacred, communal space of everyday life and longing in Jesus' name.

CONTENTS

Welcome: Dream Seeds..................................vii

Introduction..1

How-To for the Reader....................................3

1. Sitting Down Together
   With God, Partner, Family of Origin, Generative Family..................................5

2. Expectations
   Naming Your Own and Learning to Be Gentle with Yourself..................................17

3. Chores
   Doing Work at Home Together to Love Your Other Work..................................27

4. Packing Bags
   Being Prepared...Sometimes..................................37

5. Friends
   Kids Friendships and Savoring Time with Your Own Friends..................................46

6. Rest
   Sabbath in Every Season of Life..................................55

7. Rituals
   Rooting Ourselves and Kids in What Matters Most to You..................................67

WELCOME

Dream Seeds

Life accelerates and dreams become sideroads we might not take. The Dream to write a book began to germinate deep inside when my inside was not so cluttered with my own and other people's clutter. Before there was a call to seminary, a call to a congregation, a husband, a son, another son, a daughter, or dogs, there was The Dream. Long before my smile wrinkles deepened and my thighs expanded. The Dream has hibernated quietly in the dark corners of my soul.

The Dream has been named on paper and spoken aloud only a few times. Each time there was trepidation in my voice. Perhaps it sounded like tuning a guitar. After the first string is tuned with the help of a device or a human gifted with perfect pitch, the rest of the strings depend upon their neighboring strings for tuning. The tuned string is plucked first, then the untuned. The untuned string is tightened and loosened until the sound vibrations are perfectly aligned. Over and over, the untuned string aligns with the tuned string until they are each prepared to make music. The Dream has been waiting to be aligned with my life, and now, perhaps, The Dream and my life are ready to make music.

However, I could find this to be an impossible task that wreaks havoc in my life and bursts forth with out-of-tune music, in which case, at least I have a day job in a pulpit. If some background would be helpful, I am a Lutheran pastor in a denomination (branch of the Christian church) called the Evangelical Lutheran Church in American (ELCA).

Why would this wife and daughter, mom and pastor write a book? What spiritual story does this spiritual girl have to tell? Why has

The Dream continued to germinate, poking through the surface of this already full life?

Because this life of mine is not so full, after all. Perhaps John O-Donohue[1] was writing this to me:

You have traveled too fast over false ground;

Now your soul has come to take you back.

Take refuge in your senses, open up

To all the small miracles you rushed through.

It is a simple, mindless task to stay busy. I've come to gag over the word *busy*. American *busy* conjures up pride and importance. But the most destructive work of *busy* is to clutter The Dreams in the dark corners of our souls. *Busy* buries the unique desires deep within us that God needs out in the world for the sake of the common good.

For me, there are words that need to push forth, like the seedling with no choice but to sprout. Within me are words that speak to growing up in a particular family and in a particular town that I will spend a lifetime understanding. There are words that speak to accepting a call to become a pastor and staying committed to a marriage lived out around two demanding careers addressing the profound needs of people. There are words that address raising three children of whom I am fiercely proud. Each day I hope to challenge them to be their true selves, which is different from their best selves. In this very short speck of time in which I get to live, each day my work is encouraging people to be their true, imperfect, needy-for-Jesus selves.

---

[1] John O-Donohue. "For One Who is Exhausted, a Blessing." https://onbeing.org/blog/john-odonohue-for-one-who-is-exhausted-a-blessing/o. 22 Dec., 2017.

In that kind of life, weeding away our own and other people's clutter, we just might re-discover The Dream God needs out in the world. Seeds are not meant to be forgotten forever, yet they are meant to be left alone for a time. Not to be forgotten, but to sit alone in the dark until the moment the seedling pokes through the ground.

This seedling, I hope, will provide a place of shelter for women to find joy and gratitude in the everyday.

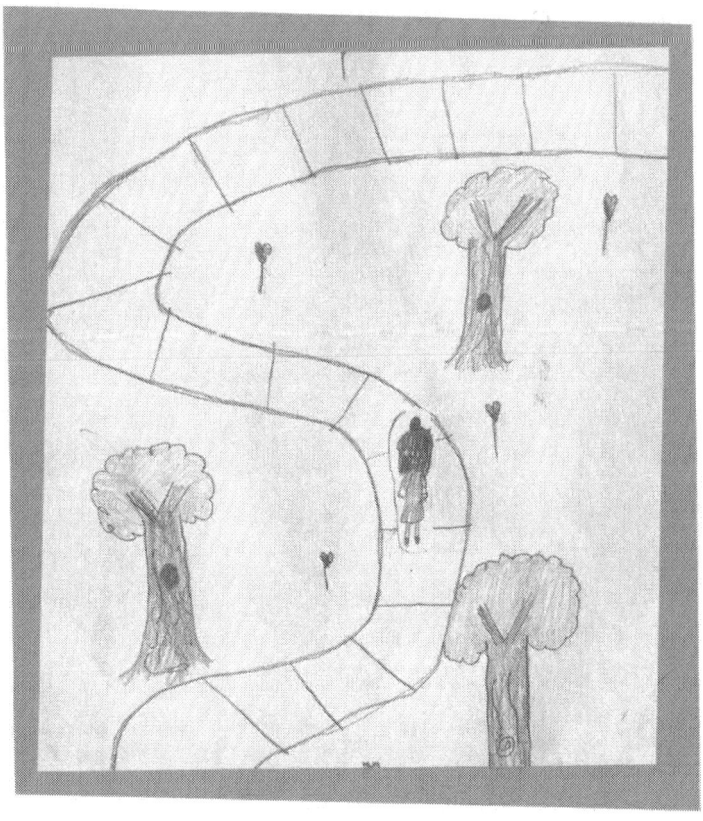

Artwork by Karis Lewton

INTRODUCTION

"Weeping may linger for the night, but joy comes with the morning."

Psalm 30:5b

Before I became a wife and a mom, I had no idea what hot tears I could weep. "I expected marriage to be as romantic as Mike and Carol Brady showed us," I thought. Tears. (This was even more hilarious when we learned Mike's sexual preference was not for Carol.) "I thought I could pull off the 'easy kid crafts' on Pinterest!" Tears. "I had no idea my boobs would leak while I'm trying to lead worship!" Tears. "I am so proud to be the mom of these kiddos I think I might die!" Tears. "Yes, I did just find a half-eaten cheeseburger under my kid's bed!" Tears.

Taking care of a now 20-year-old marriage and raising three kids ages 9, 14, and 15 has brought bucketloads of tears. There are tears of joy and tears of sadness at all hours of the day and night. Yet, when the tears from whatever part of the parade of emotions make my eyes leak, as Bob Maloogaloogaloogaloogalooga so eloquently stated, and my leaking eyes continue through the night, there is always the morning.[2]

The words of the psalmist assure us long nights and endless weeping do not last. Listen up, you teary-eyed moms. Weeping does not last! The morning faithfully comes to dry our tears and shine the light of hope and Jesus' peace. Each morning begins a

---

[2] *Big Man on Campus*. Directed by Jeremy Kagan, Regional International Pictures, 1989.

new day with new (or not new) occasions for tears and joy.

The work that brings the tears is undeniably exhausting. It demands our entire emotional and physical self while it captures years of our lives before we stop to notice. As a wife, we simply hope things will work out with our spouse, expecting the mathematical equation of more years married to equal easier years of marriage. Marriage, I have found, has gotten harder over the years as demands on our lives become more complex. As a mom, I often feel like a failure, swimming in worries that I haven't spent enough time with our kids and the time spent could have been spent better.

Marriage and raising kids is hard, guilt-ridden, sleepless work, but joy comes with the morning.

The following chapters present seven major themes that paint a picture of a woman in America who is a wife and a mom. I could say, "Moms, don't try this at home," because these stories reveal my utter lack of so much knowledge and wisdom! However, it is in the mistakes and mayhem that true life is lived. I hope these tales help you encounter encouragement and joy in whatever wild work you do.

HOW-TO FOR THE READER

Prayerfully choose a small handful of people whom you can imagine trusting with your light side and what Carl Jung described as your shadow side.[3] Invite people with whom you would be honest about the full version of who you are, including your worries and regrets, hopes and dreams.

When you first gather, it might be helpful to set the stage for trusted conversation. Promise one another your sharing will never be met with judgement. All that is said will be kept in confidence. Whatever is shared will not be spoken of outside your time together without the consent of the person who shared it.

These questions might serve to create a safe space for honest conversation:

- What recipe or Pinterest craft had you hoped would turn out differently?

- What makes you feel proud of yourself? Looking back at the family in which you grew up, what makes you feel proud?

---

[3] "The shadow goes by many familiar names: the disowned self, the lower self, the dark twin or brother in bible and myth, the double, repressed self, alter ego, id. When we come face-to-face with our darker side, we use metaphors to describe these shadow encounters: meeting our demons, wrestling with the devil, descent to the underworld, dark night of the soul, midlife crisis." Jeremiah Abrams and Connie Zweig, *Meeting the Shadow* (New York: Penguin Group, 1991), p. 3.

- Name something difficult you overcame in childhood.

- Which would you choose: a million dollars or the assurance that you will live to be at least 85 years old?

- Who is someone with whom you struggle to get along? What about that person is strikingly similar or vastly different to someone in your family growing up?

- What is something that came easy to you as a kid? Is it a part of your life today?

- What has surprised you about your own life?

- How does your Christian faith shape your days and years?

CHAPTER 1

Sitting Down Together

"When you admire people, you put them on pedestals. When you love people, you want to be together."

~ Krista Tippett[4]

"Maybe this was a bad idea," I considered once again. We had only a moment ago sat down for family game night when one sibling threw a Sorry© piece at another. (Irony noted.) It can be wonderful or unbearable to sit together. When my husband, three kids, and I sit down together, there may be laughter or hot tempers, or often a mixture of both.

Family life is not what I thought it would be. As a younger woman not yet in the thick of things, I imagined it only in heart-warming hues. I pictured the tidy sitting room of June and Ward Clever who went to sleep between crisp, ironed sheets in their own twin beds. It must be true that women's liberation led to messier homes (and shared beds).

In the thick of it, sitting down together as family can get ugly, particularly when the family includes young kids. This was news to me when I was getting used to the title "mom." There are six years between my own brother and me, unlike the 19 months between my feisty boys. I had no idea vengeful pinching was something brothers did to each other. Regularly.

---

[4] Krista Tippett, *Becoming Wise: An Inquiry into the Mystery and Art of Loving* (New York: Penguin Press, 2016), p. 83

Now I know! Now I know the photographs in glossy parenting magazines I perused in my OB-GYN's waiting room were unveiling only a slice of the story of raising kids. The magazines portrayed an adoring mother in a lovely moment and omitted the unbearable one when the glue and the glitter got out of hand or there was an unjust loss at Chutes and Ladders© and absolutely no one wants to sit down together again! (Chutes and Ladders ©, by the way, just might be the worst kids' game ever invented because of its devastating and ruinous chutes.)

Sitting down together can be risky. If my kids sit too close together in the car, for instance, mean words tumble out. Or at the dinner table after a long day, one sibling looks at his other siblings in utter shock that he is stuck forever as their relative. That's when I sit back and forecast that these kids will be assertive grown-ups who are ready for the challenge of sitting down together in other tough crowds, if only they can survive childhood around the same table.

Yet, sitting down together can be the photograph of a tidy life pasted throughout the pages of the parenting magazine. There are moments when the kind and gentle side of a child is enough to fill my heart with joy and my eyes with tears. When one sibling encourages another or helps without being asked, that moment carries enough power to erase a bad day.

For the most part, I love sitting down together with these people, my family. Sitting down together is why we are intentional about road trips and movies. Most days, we sit down together for breakfast and supper. It will not be long before these three emerging adults will sit down together with other people in places where I am not. They might live and work too far for me to join them at a table. Because time is limited, I sometimes get clever about getting them to sit together.

I might invite them to sit in the car and go grocery shopping with me and promise to buy them a donut; this works every time. Or we might not invest in cable television.

Sitting Down Together with Screens Everywhere

Someday our kids might forgive us for the "hardships" imposed on a life with no cable. Their research concludes we are literally the only family in the entire universe with only one television. On the day we started a Netflix subscription (exclusively for the wickedly cold months of winter) they thought my husband and I had been replaced by some kind of much cooler stunt doubles.

Our oldest son was about ten years old when he was having his hair cut by the woman who cut and styled mine and all my kids' hair at the time. When she asked what he liked to watch on television, he heaved a burdened sigh and clarified, "There are pictures in the living room where a television is supposed to be." (Did you know it can be tricky to hang pictures around television jacks and still balance the wall décor? This is true.)

The lone television hangs out in the basement of our home while the people mostly hang out on the main level, not straying too far from the kitchen. There will not be a television allowed in any of my kids' bedrooms, although they can find plenty of trouble on the screens of their phones before screen time's downtime sets in.

"There's so much more to do and see.
God gave you eyes for more than TV!"
~ *Mama Bear*[5]

---

[5] Stan and Jan Berenstein with Mike Berenstein, *The Berenstein Bears Discover God's Creation* (Grand Rapids: Zonderkidz, 2010).

It isn't that I worry so much about exposing them to technology or pop culture. My worry about too many screens in our home has to do with loneliness. Watching *The Office* alone is indeed funny. But watching it together with someone and later quoting Dwight when considering whether to have beets for supper, or wondering if a stapler can actually set in Jell-O, then what else might jiggle in there, too, is much more fun.

Doris Kearns Goodwin described the impact on her neighborhood in the 1950s when the first television arrived in her neighbor's living room.[6] Every evening, a few more people gathered round for baseball or the news. They were drawn out of their own living rooms to gather around a single television in one common neighborhood living room. Watching television was a communal act instead of an individualized consumption. We have one television in one room to encourage the people living under the same roof to sit down together without being attached to individual screens in all areas of the house.

"Where two or three are gathered in my name," Jesus mentioned, "I am there among them." (Matthew 18:20). Sitting down to watch *The Office* might not seem like gathering in Jesus' name. But perhaps even this holy act of sitting down together in a time when it is easy to go sit separately on our own screens is in fact gathering in Jesus' name.

For Christians, sitting down together at the Lord's Table for Holy Communion is a practice that equalizes and strengthens the community. We sit down together to receive the same meal of mercy. Each person's individual wafer and tiny cup of wine or grape juice is precisely the same. We sit down together because there is simply no other way to belong to the same community.

---

[6] Doris Goodwin Kearns, *Wait Till Next Year* (New York: Touchstone, 1997), p. 120.

In our marriage, Marcus and I do our best to sit down together, too.

Sitting Down Together in Marriage

We had been married only a few weeks the first time Marcus and I sat down together with a Marriage Care small group. It would turn out to be one of the most meaningful sit downs, sustaining us as a couple each and every year of our marriage.

We learned about Marriage Care at Luther Seminary in St. Paul, Minnesota where I was studying to be an ordained pastor. Marcus was studying to be a teacher just up the street at the University of Minnesota's St. Paul campus. Rev. Dr. William Smith was a pastoral care professor with a passion for caring for pastors' souls. He would teach us that by caring intentionally for our marriages, we care deeply for our souls. Caring for our marriage, Marcus and I would learn with other couples in the years ahead, meant we were also caring for our kids.

My husband and I signed up for a Marriage Care retreat on a Saturday with about 15 couples. We might have been the most newly married and therefore most disillusioned about a "happy marriage". With Bill and his wife, Anita, we began to see a picture of the long view of marriage.

"Good Lord," I remember thinking nervously to myself as Bill and Anita spoke about marriage. "Is marriage really this much work?"

"... the story of my marriage, which is the great joy and astonishment of my life, is too much like a fairy tale, the German kind, unsweetened by Disney."

~ Ann Patchett[7]

Turns out, it is indeed that much work! It is mostly joyful work, but to say a marriage is no work at all would lead me to wonder if one of the two partners is actually a robot and not really human.

Bill and Anita, in their full humanity, taught us the art of dialoging. Dialoging, like marriage, takes a lifetime of human practice.

Our leaders were both in their 80s and married all of their adult lives. With their white hair and Bill's trimmed white beard, they resembled Santa and Mrs. Claus, spreading marriage cheer wherever they went. They spent several minutes that afternoon dialoging about their life together. We watched, mesmerized by the love that filled their words and the mercy they freely gave away. Their marriage, too, was peppered with disappointments and hardships. They had made mistakes and would continue to make them. At the end of their dialogue, they shared a blessing by marking each other's foreheads with the sign of the cross, a Christian reminder that we are beloved and forgiven children of God through the sacrament of Holy Baptism.

And then it was our turn. Watching the Smiths was lovely, but actually test-driving dialoging seemed awkward and weird, like finding your way on the first day at a new school. Suddenly we

---

[7] Ann Patchett, *This Is the Story of a Happy Marriage* (New York: HarperCollins, 2013), p. 240.

were all in the junior high cafeteria, surreptitiously trying not to be noticed.

We were divided into groups of four couples, all of us "dialogue virgins," to stumble into the art of some of the most important learning my husband and I would ever experience together. Each partner individually answered a few simple questions in an exercise involving such topics as affirming our partner, how we communicate, or something we learned from our family of origin (the family with whom we spent the most time growing up). After writing down our individual answers on a piece of paper, we took turns around the circle dialoging with our spouse. To make sure you can picture it, one couple did the talking while the other couples did the observing.

Nothing makes a couple speak more respectfully than to be seated in a circle with three other couples observing! Dialoging in a group taught us to sit down together to listen more sharply and graciously to each other, and thereby communicate better. (I would love to say we expertly dialogue in all of our conversations, but I might as well tell you I've maintained my high school weight.)

At each of the two congregations I have served as a pastor, Marcus and I have led Marriage Care groups. Today, some of our most trusted friendships have been born out of these groups. Pastors are cautioned about making friends with people from church. These friendships can go sour if something negative happens at church, but I have broken that rule with this community of friends, with whom I would entrust my children and my deepest truths.

Even with such good practice and almost two decades of dialoging, Marcus and I manage to forget again and again how to sit down together and dialogue. Instead, I still sometimes revert to what I learned growing up. What I learned growing up was not dialoging as much as it was stewing.

Don't Be Like the Turtle

Pastors enter into people's lives at the most holy and privileged times, including preparing for marriage. The longer I serve at the congregation I am currently serving, the more privileged it becomes, as I am invited to walk with multiple generations of a family.

When I sit down with a couple for pre-marriage counseling, I assure them things will sometimes go awry, just as it always does when two human beings spend a significant amount of time together. Whatever we know about marriage is largely influenced by what we learned about marriage growing up. We learn healthy ways of being in relationship, and we learn unhealthy ways. The trick is not to plan to entirely avoid the unhealthy ways. Most likely, it is impossible to entirely avoid whatever is so deeply tucked into our beings. The trick is to watch out for the unhealthy ways that sneak up when we are stressed or tired, to be on the lookout for own our shadow side.

I discovered one of those unhealthy ways after Marcus and I made it through a couple of months of marriage. I complained to my cousin about the work of being married. My older and wiser cousin had been married for what seemed to be an eternity by then: five years. I explained my new husband just doesn't care when I am upset, and he doesn't understand how I feel. I remember summing it up like this: "Marriage kind of sucks."

What she said not only changed my perspective, it gave me a way to talk through similar tough spots with couples doing pre-marriage counseling. I also love to tell this story when I visit with someone feeling stuck in a marriage he or she has been in for a while. She explained that she and her husband had a similar tough spot early in their marriage. They would disagree, she would get mad, and then she would stew. Days might go by.

Those were the exact set of scenes playing out in my toddler-phase of marriage.

Her husband kept bugging her to talk about their disagreement and tell him why she was stewing. He began to teasingly call it the "turtle phase". Instead of addressing the problem and mutually seeking help from each other, she stuck her head in her proverbial shell and stewed. Of course, things did not get better until she emerged from the shell and talked.

Looking back to our mothers' generation, I realized the women in my family were all turtles trained to stew! I had a turtle gene that encouraged me to avoid having the needed, difficult conversation. I had learned early on to continue with life and refuse to acknowledge my need to both help and be helped. I was submerging myself in a shell like I had unknowingly been trained by the matriarchs in my life.

Once my husband also understood this, he could name my turtle phase and playfully keep me from sinking too deeply into the shell. It should surprise me that I still climb into my turtle shell even nearly two decades of marriage. But I do it because it is a place learned in the early years of my life. Now, however, I do have the tools and awareness to keep from staying inside as long.

I have also come to understand my body better, including when I am more likely to talk or more likely to hole up in my shell. "Pay attention to what your body is telling you about your own wants and needs. Find the rhythms in your cycles. There is wisdom in our biology," psychiatrist and author Dr. Julie Holland writes in her book, *Moody Bitches*[8], (an awkward title to check out at the local library.) Her book is one of the best I've ever read to help women understand the uniqueness of our bodies and what that means for

---

[8] Julie Holland, MD, *Moody Bitches: The Truth About the Drugs You're Taking, the Sleep You're Missing, the Sex You're Not Having, and What's Really Making You Crazy* (New York: Penguin Books, 2015), p. 292.

the intentional time and ways in which we sit down both alone and together.

It takes sitting down together for two partners to engage in dialogue. It cannot happen when one partner is busy pursuing a hobby and the other busy doing the laundry, or when one partner is actively raising the kids while the other is passively planted on the couch, or when one partner does all the talking and nobody listens.

Sitting down together takes intentionality. Rules may need to be agreed upon about phones so digital conversations with other people do not hinder an in-person conversation between partners. Not long ago, with some encouragement from me my husband set aside his phone for much of a Christmas break. He was purposeful not to check email on his phone. When we were out for appetizers one night, he quickly read an email he had been anticipating, and I lost it. Even though he had deliberately detached from his phone through most of the past week, one look at his phone brought out an impulsive reaction in me because I feel so strongly about how easy it is to turn to our phones and avoid deep nurturing of our relationships. I was out of line and later apologized. Even I was surprised by how quickly I became angry.

My generation of partners and parents is experiencing a moment of time when we need to step up and model eye contact to teach kids to engage in healthy conversation. Putting our distractions, such as phones or tablets, in a drawer for a few hours develops empathy and strengthen trust. Sitting down together for me means setting aside any technology that interrupts the holy work of cultivating conversation.

Sitting Down Together Moments

Sitting down together with a partner can also be risky. Ideally, there is no pinching or eye-rolling, as often happens at our family's dinner table. Those are not the real risks that accompany dialogue. "Experiencing the other side is the heart of dialogue," wrote Martin Buber. The risks of sitting down together with a spouse regard exposure. It means we honestly name whether we are in this or not. Either we are both on the side of keeping a marriage alive or we are not. Either we name our hopes, failures, and desperate need to help and be helped or we do not. Only honest dialoguing that holds nothing back paints a full picture of our own selves so that together we might create a life portrait.

For my husband and me, sitting down together at home cannot happen until the incredibly long adventure called bedtime reaches "the end." Only after all kids are mostly clean, fully fed, and nearly ready to face their fatigue can two partners reengage after the fullness of the day.

When the wild adventure finally winds down, my husband and I do sit down together nearly every night. It might be to visit over a beer or to watch an episode on Netflix (if the weather outside is frightful). We might go out for appetizers and sit on the same side of the table or enjoy the company of friends.

These moments of sitting together are meaningful because we do take time to sit down alone, too. We not only sit down together, we sit with friends of our own, or with a book, or we engage in a hobby that we do not enjoy doing together. The sitting apart, not as turtles but as whole human beings, makes the sitting together even more joyful.

Read the story of Mary and Martha in Luke 10:38-42

As Jesus and the disciples continued on their way to Jerusalem, they came to a certain village where a woman named Martha welcomed him into her home. Her sister, Mary, sat at the Lord's feet, listening to what he taught. But Martha was distracted by the big dinner she was preparing. She came to Jesus and said, "Lord, doesn't it seem unfair to you that my sister just sits here while I do all the work? Tell her to come and help me." But the Lord said to her, "My dear Martha, you are worried and upset over all these details! There is only one thing worth being concerned about. Mary has discovered it, and it will not be taken away from her." (New Living Translation)

1. How does technology help and hinder your relationship with your friends or family members?
2. Recall a heart-warming moment when you were sitting down together with family or your partner, listening as intently as Mary.
3. Dialoging with someone is risky. Is there a risk that keeps you from dialoging with your partner or closest friend? Perhaps it feels too vulnerable? You might be wrong and need to apologize? You don't want to admit you need help, like Martha admitted? Maybe you prefer to be angry instead of entering into the hard work of being honest.
4. Would you say you have a satisfying amount of time to sit alone and to sit down together with your partner? Would you like that to look different?

CHAPTER 2

Expectations

"And the gift of feminism is that we get to do all of these roles. But the problem is we can't do all of that at once."

~ *Kristen Howerton*[9]

Marcus and I had been married a mere few months when already I could see I was a prodigious wife. It was as though my wifeyness had been cracking its cocoon shell waiting to be freed until at last it was! Even though my days were busy as a full-time graduate student at Luther Seminary and I worked part-time in the seminary bookstore, I was possibly the best wife the universe had ever seen.

I bought the groceries, cooked the meals, and washed the dishes. I schlepped the laundry basket half a block down the sidewalk to the building in our seminary apartment complex where the laundry room was located. Afterward, I folded and put away the freshly washed clothes. On Saturdays, adhering to my mom's cleaning routine, I scrubbed our tiny apartment from top to bottom until the industrial tiles threatened to shine.

Yep, never had there been a more wifey-wife than me. I was made for this! I was amazing.

Several months passed. Gradually it began to dawn on me that the home I was creating was not exactly a home. In fact, our "home"

---

[9] Kate Bowler, narrator. "World's Okayest Mom". *Everything Happens*, season 5, episode 17, 11 Aug. 2020.

could easily be mistaken for a hotel designed entirely for my husband. He left for work early in the morning and returned early in the evening. He ate breakfast, and I did the dishes. He walked in the door, sat down for supper, and afterward I did the dishes. He crawled into the bed I had made that morning knowing the clothes he left in the laundry basket (if I was lucky) would soon end up back in his dresser ready for work again.

It also occurred to me that I felt deeply lonely in our marriage. I had made marriage entirely about preparing the perfect home. Unknowingly, I had given my husband permission to be a recipient of my generosity instead of a co-creator of our home. What was I doing? I was lonely and growing bitter from the over-functioning. I was tired of scrubbing the damn floor and carrying all that laundry week after week. Yet, what had I expected?

The Unchecked Expectations Cycle

Expectations tend to be sneaky. They linger around in the tall grasses of life and lunge unexpectedly. Or, to use a less slithering illustration, meet me at the kitchen sink. I am exhibiting my amazing wifey-self, making the meal and washing the dishes when bubbly, dirty dishwater splashes up in my eye and startles me with a sting.

Without realizing it, I had expected to be the perfect wife by doing all the stuff and making life super easy for my husband. I had not expected to receive the same sort of generosity. I had expected to be independent and strong. I had not expected my marriage to be a safe place of refuge for my own self. I had expected to give and not receive.

Expectations are like the redemption code hiding under the silver stuff on a gift card. They need to be exposed or they do no good. Until they are named, marital expectations slither around our feet or splash in our eyes from the dirty dishwasher.

To name your own expectations requires first to name that you are worthy of having them. You, beloved child of God, are a whole human being. Therefore, you are entitled to your own honest expectations. You, with all your cells and tissue and humanness have wants and needs of your own that do not make you weak or needy. You can only fully be your whole self if you name your relationship expectations out loud with others in the relationship.

"Expectations are resentments waiting to happen."

~ *Brené Brown quoting Anne Lamott*[10]

I would tell you it took me a very, very long time to learn this lesson, but that would imply a past tense. I continue to leave my expectations in the tall grass and push ahead while trying to conquer the endless demands of wifeyness. I mistakenly over-function and try to do it all even though there are now four people in my home, including my husband and our three kids, who are available to help.

Each time I over-function, my own expectations lead me down a bitter, impassable path. My unmet expectations, (also known as disappointments) lead to loneliness, which leads to me shutting down for a couple of days, which leads to a self-imposed distancing between my husband and me. At some point, I am ready to speak up about my disappointment with him, the only other person who can actually change the trajectory, and we reset and start again.

---

[10] Brené Brown, *Rising Strong: How the Ability to Reset Transforms the Way We Live, Love, Parent and Lead* (New York: Random House, 2017), p. 140.

This is such a predictable cycle in my life:

1. I try to do it all.
2. I feel disappointed when faced with the fact that I cannot do it all.
3. I feel bitter that I tried to do it all for too long.
4. I create distance between myself and my husband.
5. I resign not to trust him with my feelings and needs to ostensibly avoid the inevitable lonely and disappointed season, short or long as it may be.
6. Finally, I speak up and admit my needs and my husband responds every time, "Why did it take you so long to tell me?"

The Unchecked Human Limitations Cycle

We can locate a similar cycle in the Hebrew Bible. I am not the first slow learner God has ever seen when it comes to ignoring our human limitations.

Meet God's people called the Israelites. The Israelites followed and loved God, until they didn't. God had guided them and kept them safe through their wilderness hike, but sometimes the Israelites were certain they could do a better job if they took the lead and put God to the side.

They devised their own map through the wilderness using golden calves and bloody sacrifices. They did it their own way and established a distance between themselves and God...until they remembered their own way never worked. They turned around (also known as repented) and reconnected with God. "We're sorry," the Israelites honestly admitted to God. "Your way is actually the better way. Let's do that instead." God accepted their apology, and they all moved on. The Israelites followed God until they were certain they could do a better job and the cycle repeated.

Again.

And again.

Working Harder and Getting Nowhere

After two decades of marriage, I wonder how many times the cycle of my over-functioning, disappointment, distancing, and reconnection has played itself out. There are times when I blamed my husband for being too passive to see the cycle in real time. He could stop the train before it goes too far down the wrong track, I think begrudgingly, forgetting that I have just as much conducting experience as he does.

It's much easier to blame him than face my own mistakes and admit my ridiculous aversion to stating my own needs. I see this often in women when they come to visit with me as their pastor. Women sometimes sit down in my office and explain that they are fed up with the way things are with their husbands. They are fed up with their husband watching football, going fishing, and playing video games while they are doing the majority of the housework and raising kids.

When the late Edwin H. Friedman commented in a lecture that passive husbands are more determinantal to women's physical and mental health than abusive ones, I realized I see that all the time. Women push and push themselves to over-compensate for their partners. They work full-time paid jobs outside of their home, and they begin another full-time job when they arrive at home, running the house and being emotionally present for their families.

Here's the thing. I'm not so sure the problem is the men. I'm not so sure we, the women, are not contributing significantly to the problem. When I visit with the fed-up women in my office, I ask what they want their own lives to look like. In counseling terms, this is called self-defining. The conversation might go something like this:

Fed-Up Woman: "I am fed up."

Me: "Oh?"

Fed-Up Woman: "I am tired of doing all the work at home."

Me: "How do you bring that up with your husband?"

Fed-Up Woman: "It looks sort of like Mount St. Helens that day in 1980."

Me: "How does your husband respond?"

Fed-Up Woman: "He walks away and helps with nothing."

Me: "Have you ever thought about what you want your own life to look like?"

Fed-Up Woman: "My life? No, I have no time to think."

Me: "Let's give it a try. What is something you would like to be doing with your time that you don't have time to do?"

Fed-Up Woman: (long pause) "I love to bake. I love it very much and I used to bake often for my husband. But neither my husband nor my kids ever appreciate it, so I stopped. It just pisses me off when I spend hours making bread or cookies or cake and they just leave their crumbs all over the place for me to clean up and don't say thank you."

Me: "How could baking be something that you love again?"

Fed-Up Woman: "Well...I love to bake bread and give it away. Not every day, but once in a while, it warms my heart to bake a loaf of bread and deliver it to someone who just got home from the hospital, or to a friend whom I know is having a tough week. That is when baking is something I love. But it isn't as fun with kids in the kitchen fighting or my husband sulking in front of the tv."

Me: "Does your husband know you miss baking and sharing what you made?"

Fed-Up Woman: "Maybe he's forgotten. I guess I had, too. Maybe I've gotten so caught up in meeting other people's needs that I forgot I have some, too."

You can see where the rest of the dialogue might proceed. The Fed-Up Woman begins to plan how to set aside time to talk directly and alone with her husband. She will use "I" statements and begin defining what she wants her own life to look like. Weaved through conversations will be her expectations for her husband and her marriage, based on her own needs. She may need to adjust her expectations. Her kids may never fully appreciate her baking, but that should not get in the way of what she kneads, er, needs.

In any relationship between two people, we can never, ever control what the other person does or does not do. We cannot tell a person not to use his or her time a certain way without leading to resentment. We can only define who we are and where we want our own life to go and give the other person choices. Either a partner is on board or isn't. Either two partners support each other's well-being, or they don't.

Blaming is the easy out and never leads to progress. Blaming leaves you stuck on Bitter Street and you, beloved child of God, have other places to be. When Jesus promises you abundant life, he means it. Abundant life is a gift not to be squandered. It comes when you live as your whole self, honestly naming when life is not quite right. Naming your expectations does not make you needy; it makes you brave.

Entrusting Our Wellbeing to One Another

You cannot expect everything of yourself, no matter how capable you are. The way God created human beings insists upon interdependence.

Most gracious God, you have made us in your image and given us over to one another's care...

Evangelical Lutheran Book of Worship Marriage Rite[11]

Included in the liturgy of the Marriage Rite in my denomination are words about God giving us over to one another's care. I say those words very slowly at a wedding because they are breathtaking. God entrusted us to each other. What the what, God! That was a nutty idea, but it was God's idea, so we make it work.

Two people in a marriage are entrusted with each other's wellbeing. Contrary to my early wifey notions, this means both giving and receiving. It is holy work we do for one another that cannot be done if we tuck away our own needs and push ahead. Marriage at its best is filled with honesty that leads to trust that leads to intimacy. They all go hand in hand.

How God Ended the Cycle

If we say a quick hello to the Israelites before we close this chapter, we see they perpetuate the same cycle all the way through the Hebrew Bible. They trust God until they don't, then they go their own way until they return to their senses. They repent and God

---

[11] *Evangelical Lutheran Book of Worship*. (Minneapolis: Fortress Press, 2006).

forgives. Over and over again.

The cycle ends only when God puts on skin and walks Bitter Street with us. Jesus laughs, weeps, sings, and dances. He feels the very disappointments that come in any relationship with people whom we love. Jesus' death on the cross is the end of the Israelites' cycle of trust, sin, repentance. Now only forgiveness is expected.

This is good news for fed-up women. It turns out we do not actually need to be everything for all the people around us. Expectations for others and for our own selves need to be named. When we do that, we might realize what I realized at the onset of our marriage, that some of our expectations for our own selves are preposterous.

In her book *Why We Can't Sleep*[12], forty-something Ada Calhoun shares conversations with women also in their 40s who were overwhelmed and bitter about all that was expected of them. One woman, however, had come to terms with her unhealthy expectations:

"My expectations are way lower. I no longer believe that at this age I should have rock-hard abs, a perfectly calm disposition, or a million dollars in the bank. It helps to surround myself with women my age who speak honestly about their lives."

It is my greatest hope that you are finding comfort in the collective naming of our expectations as you read this book. We expect so much of ourselves in our marriage, in our paid work, in administrating our homes, in taking care of kids and parents and partners. My spiritual director has asked me if I'm trying to put Jesus out of business. He has to remind me that Jesus' death is enough. I need not expect to take care of everything when Jesus

---

[12] Ada Calhoun, *Why We Can't Sleep: Women's New Midlife Crisis* (New York: Grove's Press, 2020).

has taken care of the most important thing.

Forgiveness means I am free to simply live. God does not expect me to run myself down and try to be the Savior of myself and others. I am free and you are free to live as a reflection of Jesus' grace and mercy. You will not always get it right, and then you need to speak up and be honest about your expectations, so that you may live as your whole self. Then leave the dirty dishes. Your kitchen does not need to be perfect, and neither do you.

Read Jesus' words for those who are overburdened from Matthew 11:28-30.

"Are you tired? Worn out? Burned out on religion? Come to me. Get away with me and you'll recover your life. I'll show you how to take a real rest. Walk with me and work with me—watch how I do it. Learn the unforced rhythms of grace. I won't lay anything heavy or ill-fitting on you. Keep company with me and you'll learn to live freely and lightly." (The Message translation)

1. In what parts of your life do you feel overburdened? What contributes to this feeling?
2. Can you recall a time when you were honest with yourself and with someone you love about your expectations? What was it like to be so vulnerable?
3. Ada Calhoun concluded her research with a note of grace and mercy: "Listening to other women's stories this year has given me confirmation, finally, that our expectations have been absurd. So many women I spoke with-- objectively successful women--felt ashamed of their perceived failures. What if we're not failures? What if what we've done is good? At any rate, maybe it's good enough." How might you resonate with her conclusion?

CHAPTER 3

Chores

"Women run the small country called Home, millions of us do it in our spare time, and no one who doesn't run that small country really knows what it feels like in the dead of night when the task lists jitter like tickertape through your seething brain."

~ *Allison Pearson*[13]

One evening after supper when my kids were between the ages of 4 and 11, I immediately and uncharacteristically plopped down on the couch. I had made the meal and enjoyed it with my family at the table. Typically, I traveled from the table directly to the kitchen sink to wash the dishes. As though my busybody self had been taken over by a leisurely alien, I sat down on the couch and began to read a book.

This was not my idea. My husband had encouraged me to learn to sit down and depend more on my kids. They had been doing chores all their lives, but I usually hovered around and nonchalantly re-wiped the table and grimaced at the dirty dish that had been "washed."

On the night I sat with my book, I perused the kitchen full of my kids and balked that my family can do stuff without me! Sitting down and relinquishing the workload for the evening empowered

---

[13] Allison Pearson. "I Don't Know How I Did It All Those Years". *The Telegraph*. 9 Sept. 2011.
https://www.telegraph.co.uk/culture/film/8753201/Allison-Pearson-I-dont-know-how-I-did-it-all-those-years.html

my kids to demonstrate what it is to be family.

From my perspective, there has been no more challenging time to be a mom in the United States than these days. The expectations are simply unrealistic that a woman might work her butt off doing some kind of paid or unpaid work during the day, manage a home, and be genuinely present for a partner and kids. Oh, and self-care is something we are "supposed" to do, too.

When my nephew was a few years old, my mom asked him what he would like for Christmas. He listed roughly 12 toys he hoped his doting grandma might deliver and then brightly concluded, "And that's all!" To him, his list was not so long. However, what was just a few items to him was actually *quite* a few, even for a doting grandma!

The list of what a mom is expected to do reminds me of my nephew's Christmas list. Moms work and raise kids and that's all! The people at your work see what you do at work. The people at your home see snippets of what you do at home. Only you see all of it. And only you see how poorly you might be taking care of your own body and soul.

It Is a Long List

As I mentioned in the previous chapter, when women visit with me struggling with feeling overwhelmed and overloaded at home and work, it is clear we have set unrealistic expectations for ourselves. Frequently, we are our own worst enemies. We enable passive partners, over-function for our kids, and take whatever meager amount of time and energy we might have leftover to dedicate toward self-care.

> When you care about something, you try to do it well. When you care about everything, you do nothing well.
>
> ~ *Kendra Adachi*[14]

In my life, when I have reached my limit because I allowed the list to get too long, I stop and wonder about the expectations. Who expects me to do all the things on this endless list? Is it someone else, or is it really just me? My husband expects me to sit down sometimes, my kids expect me to be present, and my work expects me to be a healthy and faithful pastor. (I realize this is not a shared expectation among all churches.) It is only me who expects myself to do all the things day after day. No one else, just me. The work of a mom today can be intensely difficult to define. We probably need to take a break from our chores and sit down in order to do it.

Hovering Moms in the Sacristy

I noticed a shift at church with junior high confirmation students in a space at church called the sacristy. The sacristy is a place of preparation located next to a sanctuary. Think of it like the basement at Downton Abbey where the small group of spunky workers congregate to get ready for the big meal. In the sacristy, Holy Communion is prepared and the people leading worship prepare, too. The worship leaders include seventh graders who carry the processional cross and assist with the offering and Holy Communion.

On Sunday mornings, worship leaders wear robes known in fancy

---

[14] Kendra Adachi. *The Lazy Genius Way: Embrace What Matters, Ditch What Doesn't, and Get Stuff Done* (Colorado Springs: Waterbrook, 2020), p. 12.

church talk as albs. We wear albs in order to keep the focus on worship and not on the attire of the leaders. If it sounds simple to don an alb, you've never tried it! This is no fuzzy bathrobe. There are buttons surreptitiously placed and you put on the robe over your clothes in front of strangers, and it's just a weird thing we do. To top it off, we tie a rope called a cincture around our waste using a specific knot and sliding the knot to our left hip. The whole thing is overwhelming the first few times, but there are several gracious adults (who also periodically struggle with their albs and cinctures) who are always ready to help.

In the last few years, I have noticed a few parents trailing into the sacristy with their 7th grade child. Okay, not so much parents as moms. They hover around the alb closet, help with the buttons, and stare quizzically at the cincture.

My colleague made a genius move and gently explained to parents that they are uninvited into the sacristy. We hope the church is a place kids can discover how much support they have in their lives, including among adults who help them prepare for worship. Observing the change, kids are often relieved to be freed of their hovering moms (sorry moms, we are often the problem). There is great pride when a seventh grader finds all the buttons and nails the cincture knot! The next time it is their turn to help lead worship, they confidently stroll to the alb closet knowing they've got this, and then help a fellow 7th grader tying and untying their cinctures.

As a mom who regularly issues the most basic, obvious reminders to her kids, I do understand why moms hover in the sacristy. We want our kids to be comfortable. I am a hoverer, too.

When one of my kids was in 6th grade, my mom and I were watching him long jump at a track meet. Between jumps, he walked over to where we were sitting to say hi to us. (Okay, he was actually looking for food.)

"Do you need to go to the bathroom before you jump again?" asked this hovering mom to her long jumping middle schooler.

Afterward, my mom kindly pointed out I needed to land the chopper. "Did you really ask him if he had to go the bathroom? Good Lord, can't he figure that out on his own?"

Awkward pause. "Yes, he can," said not my voice but my expression, realizing what a hovering question I'd asked my son. The truth is, I carry around an abundance of those *helpful* questions. "Did you pack a snack?" "Brush your teeth?" "Take a shower?" Asking so many those helpful questions, it turns out, might not be the most helpful.

"No one's work is done until everyone's work is done."

In my house, when I am most overwhelmed by the workload at home, I am usually the problem. In my efforts to "be helpful," I carry the stress that belongs on the shoulder of my own kids and sometimes even my spouse. My list is too long because my expectations are off. I have chosen accommodating over challenging. It seems I have the ability to get this wrong on a daily basis.

> Increasing one's threshold for others' pain can help them mature. Sometimes the most truly 'caring' response might be to allow people to experience sufficient pain that their responses have the maturing effect of making them more responsible.
>
> ~ Rabbi Edwin Friedman[15]

In family systems therapy, we talk about this in terms of pain tolerance. While chores are not physically painful, they can be a pain in the butt. However, chores are part of belonging in a family, therefore, it is important for me to "share the pain" with my kids and spouse. It is not my job as a mom to make my kids' lives easy. Sometimes, my job is to cheer them on and let life be a little hard, as long as they are safe. Yes, doing the dishes sucks when you just want to scroll through your favorite social media app. Yes, putting away your laundry may not be your favorite way to spend a Sunday afternoon. Yes, working with your sibling to clean the garage might be less desirable than going to the dentist.

"No one's work is done until everyone's work is done." I heard myself saying this to my kids not long ago. I wasn't sure where it came from, but it seemed a familiar phrase that captured what I hope my kids will understand about chores.

Recently, I was at a retreat at Camp Metigoshe with a friend and fellow Bible camp counselor from years ago. We were putting away the dishes. She playfully said, "No one's work is done until everyone's work is done," and the recesses of my brain cheered. I had learned that phrase when I was a counselor with her at Camp Metigoshe! We would dig into the chore list at the end of an exhausting week with wild and adventurous campers. Cleaning

---

[15] David W. Cox, *"The Edwin Friedman Model of Systems Thinking: Lessons for Organizational Leaders"*, 2006, http://uulead.org/docs/family-systems.pdf

outhouses, washing down mattresses, sweeping and scrubbing. We were so tired from pouring our hearts into our work with campers, but we knew the expectation: "No one's work is done until everyone's work is done." As any camp counselor in the history of Bible camps will tell you, this is what community looks like.

The Best Answer May Be a Shrug

Not long ago, my family went on vacation out of the country for the very first time. We had chosen the experience of a special vacation over Christmas presents and had been waiting and waiting for this occasion. Two days before we left, I came down with the flu. It changed its mind from the flu to a cough and back again. When the moon came out, so would my fever. It would disappear with the sun. I had run myself so thin at work and home to get ready for our highly-anticipated vacation, my body revolted and insisted on lying down.

I was mostly packed, except for the last few items I add to a suitcase, such as underwear. Have you ever traveled out of the country only to realize you forgot all of your underwear? Yeah, don't do that.

When we arrived at our destination, I had completely lost my voice. I could whisper inaudibly, but that was more annoying than helpful. When we got off the plane, one of my kids asked, "How much longer until we're at the hotel?" I shrugged my shoulders. "What do we do when we go through customs?" Shoulder shrug. "Where do we get our bags?" Shrug. After a few more shrugs, I thought to myself, "This. Is. Awesome!" I couldn't help anyone; I could only let me kids try to answer their own nonurgent questions. Everyone was just fine, even though I could not utter a syllable. It was one of my favorite moments of that trip.

Handing Over the Soup Spoon

The truth is, kids are capable of much more than we might challenge them to do. From the moment they emerge from the birth canal, kids are tough. If my own kids can be savvy on social media, they can be savvy with their daily work at home. They can cook and clean. They can solve problems and make decisions. They can fight like maniacs, and they can follow the camp mantra: "No one's work is done until everyone's work is done."

When I am worn out and even resentful about how much work there is to do at home, I recite my favorite psalm, Psalm 63. "Oh God, you are my God, and I will ever praise you. My soul thirsts for you, my flesh faints for you, as in a dry and weary land where there is no water."

Some days, the work at church and home leaves me in a weary land where there is no water. I grow resentful and bitter at my spouse and my kids. But exactly no one has assigned me the work of doing everyone else's work. That expectation is my own and can be laid to rest for the good of me and my family.

When I began my call as a senior pastor a few years ago, my husband and I had many conversations about what this new call meant for our family. He was supportive of my call to lead a congregation we had grown to love and call home. Yet I simply could not carry on with the same responsibilities at home and do the work I wanted and needed to do at church.

After brainstorming together, we agreed he would handle the cooking on weekends. He had cooked sporadically before that, with specialties like venison stew and pheasant chili. When he did cook he enjoyed it. It was not something he did often only because our routine was for me to do the cooking.

Since I began my call five years ago, he is the weekend cook who tries to stretch the meal into the week with leftovers to lighten my load in the kitchen. Now, he looks forward to cooking on the weekends. It is one of his greatest joys; he will tell you. He enjoys the solitude and purpose of preparing the meal, filling the table with meat and potatoes or something else he loves to make. ("Soup. It's always soup!" one of our kids once said.) Our kids look forward to sitting down at a table covered in his cooking. They now know it is possible to cook chicken and pork that isn't totally dry, which is the only way I really know how to cook those things. Their palates have expanded, and food is something we really enjoy sitting down together to eat on weekends. Cooking is a joy and a gift of my husband, and we would not have known that if he and I had not come to that arrangement together and changed our established routine. I had to hand over the soup spoon and stay out of the kitchen.

Even after 20 years, my husband and I still wrestle with which responsibilities belong to whom at home. It has never been easy for us to balance our paid work with how to accomplish our work at home. We do our best to teach our kids how to share the chores with us, but it is still hard.

Marriage, however, is a partnership, and partnership requires sharing the chores. It means things might not get done right away or in the same way I would do them. It means holding my tongue and saying thank you, thank you, thank you. And please, please, please. And no one's work is done until everyone's work is done. And sometimes, a tired mom's work is to sit down and read a book.

Read these proverbial words from an ancient teacher.

"There is nothing better for mortals than to eat, drink, and find enjoyment in their toil." Ecclesiastes 3:24

1. What toiling chore do you never avoid because it gives you joy? Why might that be?

2. If you could ease out of one particular chore at home, how might you spend that time instead?

3. How can you lovingly practice teaching your family "No one's work is done until everyone's work is done," as a way of empowering your kids and strengthening your marriage?

CHAPTER 4

Packing Bags and Bags (and Bags)

A mom to her husband at their daughter's baptism: "Did you pack the diaper bag?"

Husband to wife wearing a smirk of pride: "Yes, I did."

Wife to husband, desperately needing a clean diaper for the baby being baptized in 20 minutes: "Where is it?"

Husband with no smirk and starting to pale: "It's at home. You told me to pack it, not to bring it."

Wife: silence, displaying admirable self-restraint

"Every day is an adventure," I find myself saying every day I am overwhelmed by the adventure.

Life as a mom and a wife is an intense day-to-day and week-to-week adventure for which exactly no one is perfectly prepared. No day or week is precisely the same, just as no two children are the same. Each child emerges as a new and unique character in a family's story and requires new and unique learning from parent and guardians. Whatever we learn raising the first child does not prepare us for everything we need to know to raise future siblings.

Each of us is caught up in such a grand and unpredictable adventure. We are living out God's story in the world by taking care of the people and places God has entrusted to us with no manual or clear set of instructions. One of the first stories the Bible tells is the moment God created human beings. It was God's own, divine adventure, scooping up newly-invented dirt, taking a deep breath, and letting it all out. This is how humans were formed, made from nothing more than what God happened to have lying around.

Did God really intend to create us out of dirt, of all things? Was this a spur-of-the-moment decision by God? "Oh! I need to make people, and I forgot the ingredients in my bag back home. Oops! Let's see. What else do I have around? Radiating stars? Pristine blue ocean water? Guess I'll just use some dirt."

God created humans, although God may not have been prepared for the migraines we humans would incite. God handed humans over to depend on each other. My family depends on me to be the one who invariably knows what the heck is going on. I am entrusted with the almighty calendar.

One Diaper Bag at a Time

On the weekends, I prepare for the adventure of the upcoming week by filling the family whiteboard calendar with practices, meetings, games, events, and a meal plan. I'm not excited about color-coordinating, so I use a black, green, or red Expo marker depending on which marker has not been discovered and thereby destroyed by an exuberant young artist. I hide good markers like some people hide cash or good whiskey.

I have appreciated the weekly calendar practice because it eliminates the annoyance of the other four people in my house taking turns asking me, "What are we doing today?" They can read the calendar, and the calendar won't get snippy with the repetition of the question.

Taking life one week at a time is a nice relief from the days my kids were little and we lived hour-to-hour, one diaper and diaper bag refill at a time. Every trip outside our home required packing a bag.

Even a quick trip necessitated a diaper bag because what if I am only grabbing a jug of milk in the grocery store and someone who has been constipated for days poops his pants halfway through the freezer section and I have to stand in the check-out line pretending my own kid isn't actually with me.

And so, moms pack bags. In case someone has an accident, in case someone is suddenly on the edge of death due to hunger, in case that one special toy is needed to calm a screaming someone, in case a kid has found a sucker at the bottom of another bag and now has tissues glued to half his face and needs a wet wipe like Homer Simpson needs a beer. It is better to pack the bag and be prepared, just in case.

A bag might hold the key to getting through that one intense moment which for me, always happened at the grocery store. When my kids melted down all at once or took turns and even I, who had seen a million meltdowns, was not prepared for the helpless humiliation, wanting to disappear into the freezer with the frozen dough because I thought I was prepared and alas, I was not.

"We live with mystery, but we don't like the feeling. I think we should get used to it. We feel we have to know what things mean, to be on top of this and that. I don't think it's human, you know, to be that competent at life."

~ *Mark Strand*[16]

---

[16] Mark Strand. "The Art of Poetry, No. 77." *the PARIS REVIEW*. Issue 148, Fall 1998, https://www.theparisreview.org/interviews/1070/the-art-of-poetry-no-77-mark-strand.

On the Myers Briggs Type Indicator©, I land firmly in the "J" category, which means being prepared is important to me. "J" is short for "Judging," describing a person as orderly and structured. I am a list maker to the extent that I cannot comfortably leave my office on a Friday without a list at the ready for the following week.

As best I can, I plan each week at work and at home *in order* (see how I did that?) to know what to expect. I can be prepared and ready for whatever madness comes. But wait, what is that you are trying to utter through muffled laughter, Real Life? You sound like Sarah hiding around the corner when Abraham was visiting with the angel. "Ridiculous and impossible," you say?

Attempts at the Ridiculous and Impossible

On a Saturday morning not long ago, I planned to wake up slowly. Maybe I would work out but probably not. I would curl up on the comfy living room chair and read a book before going to the office early and knock a few simple tasks off my list when the building would be quiet.

Exactly none of that happened. None.

I bolted out of bed at 4:00 a.m. when our puppy sounded a piercing bark alarm from his kennel at the sight of the neighborhood meddling cat, who enjoys gingerly climbing up the porch to gaze menacingly at him from the window. Once I convinced him to knock it off since the cat could eat him for an early morning snack, he returned to his slumber, and I retired back to bed.

Before 6:00 a.m., my daughter woke up to collect the nice, warm puppy and curl up in her own bed. The puppy, more interested in frolicking than cuddling, sprinted to my husband and my bed and instructed us by the digging of his nose in our faces to get up, already!

This was not the plan, humans and animals! By 7:00 a.m. I was crabbily assisting in the cutting and tying of a fleece-tie blanket for a Christmas gift (irony noted) under the direction of the seven-year old, avoiding the big brown eyes of the oblivious and content puppy.

Of course, a Saturday morning with kids and a puppy would not go as planned. Shouldn't I know better by now than to formulate a plan for a Saturday morning? It is predictable that a kid who can sleep in will not, and puppies who look adorable while sleeping will default to rambunctious whenever a peaceful opportunity arises.

Every day is an adventure, and adventures by their nature tend not to go precisely as planned. Adventures challenge the calendar and the organized meal plan. They defy the logic of "everything I need is in the diaper bag." The thing you need (or the diaper bag itself) may have been left at home.

No Time to Pack a Bag

So long ago in a place known as the wilderness, the people of God known as the Israelites were wandering. They had little idea where they were going and no idea how to get there. Prepared they were not. They knew only two things:

- A. God had freed them from the slavery imposed upon them by the Pharaoh of Egypt.
- B. God was leading them to a place God called the Promised Land, but they were in such a hurry when they left, they could bring no bag.

What the Israelites who wandered through the wilderness did *not* know was simple:

Where they were going and when they would we get there.

There was no map nor itinerary for this adventure. Because of the danger that pursued them when they left their homes in Egypt, there was no time to pack a bag. Meals were served only when God showered bread and quail from the sky in the mornings. It did not matter whether they were picky eaters and disliked quail. The limited knowledge the Israelites held was that God would take them where God needed them to go. They would arrive bagless when God needed them to stop wandering.

Much of our days are for wandering, even if our calendar is there to direct us. Sometimes unremarkably and sometimes with fervor, we wander from home to work and back again, with activities on our calendar in between. We do our best to prepare when we pack purses and busy bags for the car, bags for work and bags for the pool. We do not know how long we might be healthy enough to do it, or how long life will stay this way. We only know what the Israelites knew: that God leads us where God needs us to go when God needs us there, prepared or not.

Unlike me, God is not a "J" on the Myers Briggs.

Surprisingly, however, when I was pregnant with each of our three kids, Marcus and I chose not to learn the sex of the babies. The "J" side of me rolled over and didn't care. We bought and received clothes that donned neutral colors. The nursery was themed in Paddington Bear, Noah's Ark, or cute and cuddly monkeys.

Not knowing made the nine months of waiting a more beautifully mysterious adventure. Not knowing exactly for whom we were preparing heightened the anticipation and the joy. In the delivery room, we explained to the nurses beforehand we wanted Marcus, not the doctor, to tell me the sex. It is one of our favorite moments in the book of our marriage: with each delivery of our children, his frantic and teary glance and then his announcement to me with tears spilling out of his hazel eyes.

There is simply no preparing for a moment like that.

Packing the Bag and Forgetting It at Home

On a warm summer day many Augusts ago, my oldest son (raising the oldest is always an experiment, right?) and I drove to our church for day camp, a weeklong adventure at our church. Enthusiastic young adult counselors led the week with stories, games, and songs around a particular theme or Bible story.

This day was a special day during the week called Splash Day! The day promised water fun like a slip and slide and splash games. I had helped my very independent five-year-old pack his lunch bag along with a bag for his towel, sunscreen, and swim trunks to prepare for the day.

When we pulled into the church parking lot for Splash Day, we had a problem. He had remembered his lunch bag but not his swim bag. Oh dear. These are moments of truth for a mama. Do I:

- A. Rush home to retrieve his bag to save him from missing Splash Day?
- B. Use this moment to help him learn packing a bag must be followed by bringing the bag along?

I chose the latter. I explained to my otherwise quite organized child, "I'm sorry you forgot your bag, but I don't have time to go home and get it." It was tough, but mostly the only option. My work morning was full enough that it would have required some race car driving to retrieve the bag.

It is possible he hasn't forgotten a bag since. (Sadly, this exercise does not work for my other two kids.)

Later I wondered whether the disappointment of missing Splash Day was memorable for my son. Did he despair long? Does he have bitter feelings regarding the way I handled it? I recently asked him if he remembered the day at camp when he forgot his swim bag and missed out on Splash Day. "What?" He replied, after a moment of consideration. "I don't remember that."

Therapy session averted.

Trusting in the Guide, Not the Map

Every day is an adventure. It takes courage to go out into the adventure when we cannot be prepared for most of what happens. We cannot be ready for the deep disappointments at work or the sad surprises in our family. The pain of seeing the hurt our kids experience from a friend or someone else will catch us off guard every time. We cannot prepare for those days, weeks, or months we find ourselves disconnected from our partner.

"We pray to God from where we are, not from where we consider we should be. And God, who knows us where we are, can lead us to where we can be."

~ *Terrence Fretheim*[17]

I imagine this is why God kept the Israelites in the dark about what was coming next: Not because God is anti-preparing, but because a true wilderness adventure tends to require a guide more than a map. Instead of depending on their own skills and sense of

---

[17] Terrence Fretheim, *Creation Untamed: The Bible, God, and Natural Disasters*, (Grand Rapids, MI: Baker Academics), 2010, p. 142.

direction, the Israelites could depend only on the guide, on the God who sent them into the wilderness so God could lead them to new life.

I love the practice of preparing and the sense of being ready. Yet I know everyday life does not unfold in the right order. Instead, God tells us not to fear, promising to walk with us through overwhelming wilderness. We might not know what comes next, but we are assured God has already packed all the mercy we need to get us there.

Read Proverbs 16:9 about planning and living.

"We plan the way we want to live, but only God makes us able to live it."
(The Message Translation)

1. How do you prepare for the day or the week? Why do you think that is your approach?
2. Think of a time when being unprepared was what was best?
3. How can you be gentler with yourself about preparing and being unprepared?

CHAPTER 5

Friends

"Happiness is what you notice."

~ *My dear friend, Audrey*

We cradled steaming cups of coffee and inhaled the crisp, spring morning air as we sat a few feet apart on a wooden bench. On Wednesdays before our families shed their pajamas, we drove our 2019 Steel Saphire Honda Pilots to a park. If genuine friendship is reflected in owning the exact same make, model, and color vehicle, then that is indeed what we have going on here.

The pandemic in 2020 made it tricky to sit down with a friend. As you already know from chapter one, I am a fan of sitting together. Previously, my friend, Audrey, and I had met regularly at a coffee spot. Her profession as an OB-GYN and mine as a pastor overlap in the category of caring for people. She listens to people's pain and cares for their bodies. I listen to a different variety of people's pain and care for their souls.

After a few months of quarantining, we were determined to visit safely and stay connected. A pandemic, we all now know, simultaneously challenges gatherings and makes them more necessary than ever. The infamous year unfolded unnaturally. Headlines shouted impeachment, pandemic, racism, political division, anger over wearing cloth masks (in my own corner of the world more than anywhere else), and as each layer unfolded, I needed this human connection more and more.

There was much to process over steaming cups of coffee in "The

Year of Absurdity," as my friend Glen entitled it. Audrey and I needed to talk through being white, privileged, and supported women when the stories of our sisters in Christ who are black and brown were finally breaking through. We needed to talk through the impending dangers of living in rural America with some of the world's highest pandemic-related mortality rates. How do we parent through it? How do we care for our own souls through it?

I could honestly tell my friend what made me very pissed off, what worried me, and what made me cry. Sometimes she needed to rant and other times it was me. Sometimes I unloaded my deep sadness and other times it was her. Most of the time, we got back in our twinsie cars more hopeful and peaceful about our lives and our world. Other times, we each carried a piece of the anxiety, knowing our lives and this world are not always fine. There is peace in being *not fine* with a friend, perhaps there is even happiness if we stop to notice.

How Many Friends Does a Grown-Up Need?

I am 42 as I write these words. I can count on one hand how many people I consider to be dear and trusted friends. Rarely have those five changed over the years. I have no dear friends from childhood, one from college who comes and goes, and a seminary friend whom I rarely see, yet when we get together, it is always as if no time has passed.

This one handful of friends showed up when I needed them in my life, as God tends to work out. God brings the right people at the right time. While I have organized many playdates for my kids over the years, none of my sacred friendships were premediated. No one set us up, and it would not have appeared to me that we had enough in common to create such adhesive relationships.

One friend, Terry, was my boss two decades ago at the seminary bookstore. Our love for words and books and his genuine joy for life inspires me week after week. This inspiring friend of mine writes me an email each Tuesday morning. I can look forward to at least one encouraging and interesting email to welcome me back to work after my Mondays off.

"A day without a friend is a like a pot without a single drop of honey left inside."

~ *Winnie the Pooh*

Another friend, Brice, is a pastor at Oak Grove Lutheran Church in Richfield, Minnesota where I interned. Almost every month since then, he has called me to pray and provide spiritual direction. His wisdom and grace keeps me grounded in the often ungrounding work of life as a pastor, mom, and wife.

A common denominator among these friends is their curiosity about life. Like me, these are human beings who are not trying to arrive at anything, but simply to be. They are who they are, moving through life with an open mind and a sense of wonder for the Spirit's work in it. They have shown me unconditional love and given me permission to be fully me.

Grown-Up Friendship

In one conversation with Pastor Brice, I was in a tough spot in my marriage. It was a lonely season for me. As a pastor, there are very few people with whom I can honestly confide about such seasons. Brice had planned to call me, but I texted and told him I couldn't talk that day. I was too sad, and I didn't want to spend his time crying on the phone. He texted back and encouraged me to call him anyway.

I considered. It seemed like a bad idea. I cry alone, usually in my closet with the door closed. Then I wash my face and reemerge tear-free.

But that day, I looked at Brice's text and thought about all the years of conversations behind us and how well this person knows me. My tears would not scare him away. He is well aware of who I am, so I called him. And I cried. Our conversation was mostly me crying. I had never cried like that on the phone before. The tears ran particularly hot because I was in my office at church. In my office, I am the one who counsels others through their tears, but in that moment, the tough spot poured from my eyes. I was embarrassed for only a moment, and then I forgot to be embarrassed and continued to cry.

It is sacred space when a friend simply lets you cry. My friend did not try to fix it or tell me it will all work out. He sat quietly on the other end of the phone and provided holy ground for a most vulnerable act. My tears, not words, were the healing balm I needed.

Our Kids' Friendships

Friendship can be a slow evolution or a quick connection. It seems to perpetuate through face-to-face or digital interactions. Love has no end, Paul wrote in 2 Corinthians 13. Love, including the friendship kind, is not bound by any criterion or how we interact. Friendship only requires interaction.

"The usual interactions of older-younger, richer-poorer, smarter-dumber, male-female even, cease to matter. You meet with a clean slate every time, and you meet on equal terms. Anything may come of it or nothing may. That doesn't matter either. Only the meeting matters."

~ *Fredrick Buechner*[18]

For moms, this often means we schedule playdates for our kids. Because the meeting matters, we network with other moms or dads to initiate meetings for our kids. We hope these meetings will teach kids to share their Legos© and practice manners. They also allow moms to affirm the manners of other kids (because kids behave best at other people's houses) and passive-aggressively encourage our own kids to have better manners. (Wasn't that so nice that Billy hung up his jacket.)

I have always assumed a mom is tasked with being nosy about friends. Friends have an unbearable amount of influence on the choices kids make, which leads me to ask often in the least nosy tone I can muster: "Who did you sit by at lunch today?" "Who do you suppose you Snapchat the most?" "Who else is on your Xbox game?"

I grew up in such a small town that my own mom always knew who I was with. She never needed to ask me! Sometimes she would ask another mom, which once got me into trouble when I was not with the friend I told her I was with. Nary was there a dumber kid than the one who fibbed to her mom in a small town. In a small town you have not one mom, but dozens of them.

If you are naturally a follower, a pleaser or a helper (#2 in the

---

[18] Frederick Buechner, *Whistling in the Dark: A Doubter's Dictionary* (San Francisco: Harper One, reprint edition, 1993), p. 55.

Enneagram) you need to be intentionally in conversation with your kids. Kids inherit these parts of us and may be inclined to follow, please, or offer to be too helpful with their friends.

Laying out possible scenarios is one way to crack open a conversation with kids about friends. Cater to your kid's age. When my kids were younger, I might have asked, "What happens if you are with your friends and they want to watch something on their tablets you know you could not watch at home?" Or to older kids, "What might you do if you are at school and someone wants you to try a new vape flavor?" Cater the question to what you know they will face. Not sure? Ask a school counselor. They are the wise sages you need in your kids' teenage lives. They will tell you the truths about the world your kid lives in and doesn't want you to know.

In these conversations, I offer my kids one fool-proof way out. When they find themselves in a sticky situation, this may be their ace-in-the-hole. If they feel unhealthy peer-pressure, they can tell their friends I'm the world's most deplorable mom. "I can't watch that show, vape that flavor, or whatever it might be" because their wicked non-step mom will take their phone and everything they love away until they move out of the house or start paying rent. Their friends don't need to know that's an exaggeration. If it loosens the peer pressure, I'll gladly play the part of world's worst mom. You might not want that starring role, so you can tell your kids to pretend they are sick and ask to go home. That may work, too.

Jesus' Sermon on Friendship

We can tell our kids that real friends won't put them in those positions, but real friends are only human. My kids' friends are also learning about life. I would rather do all that I can to equip my kids for those tough spots than expect my kids to avoid them. Kids live in a messy world, and I can never protect them from it, but I can hope to talk through life with them enough to teach them to define their own beliefs and boundaries. And I can love them through it all the way.

This seems to me the kind of love Jesus offers his friends. Jesus is verbose about friendship in chapter 15 of John's gospel, which is part of Jesus' Farewell Discourse. Throughout most of chapters 13-17, Jesus is preparing the disciples, whom he calls his friends, for the crucifixion. The disciples do not yet know how it will play out. They cannot comprehend Jesus' partly enigmatic and partly explicit message about the end of his life.

Until Good Friday happens, Jesus' friends will not understand most of what he says, which is often true with our kids. They can catch bits and pieces of what we say to prepare them for life without parents or guardians close by, but only when they arrive at the moment of peer pressure, heartbreak, or grief do they fully understand what is at stake. Their health, their safety, their virginity, their values, their relationships are all ambiguous until the moment they are not. Parenting kids is constant preparation and practice for independent and real life.

Jesus tells his own friends that they are only his friends if they do what he tells them, which is to love one another. Friendship is living out Jesus' command to love one another. That might mean telling a friend no, you are not ready to watch that show, or to experiment with vaping. It might mean telling a friend it's okay to cry, even if crying with others isn't your thing. Or it may look like typing encouraging words in an email, or processing 21st century racism against black and brown bodies over steaming cups of dark roast.

Love is how Jesus has taught us to interact, making it crystal clear that human connection is absolutely necessary for survival. We require the connection of friends to make sense of life and our place in it.

Can Your Spouse Be Your Best Friend?

With couples preparing for marriage, it's common for them to tell me with pride they are marrying their best friend. I know couples who have been married for many years who would say the same lovely thing. I believe them. Your spouse can be your best friend.

Trouble comes when your spouse becomes your only friend. When you depend on your spouse to help you process work problems, your body image, your parenting issues, your hopes and dreams, and your schedule, it is too much. You have put too much pressure on your spouse to accommodate that vast array of information.

In our lives, we need a more diverse repertoire of people. At different seasons in life, we need a therapist, an exercise buddy, a Bible study or book club, a marriage enrichment group, family, or even one good, solid friend to whom we are not married. One spouse cannot be expected to fulfill all the roles.

For example, my spouse and I do not understand racism with the precisely same lens. I (most of the time) understand I am not right and he is wrong, or the other way around. I appreciate his difference of opinion for the reason that it helps me clarify mine. However, we do not spend excessive amounts of time talking about racism because it can leave both of us feeling slightly annoyed at each other.

So, I reserve most of those conversations for my coffee visits with Audrey on the wooden bench. She can tell me to chill out or to spell out what I'm trying to think through. At the end of our conversation, our friendship is not defined by what we discuss but only by the abundant connection offered each week.

Read Ephesians 3:14-19. The writer of this letter encourages others in their faith. As these words are meant to encourage Christian faith, they also reveal a deep love for one another, as is offered in friendship.

For this reason I bow my knees before the Father, from whom every family in heaven and on earth takes its name. I pray that, according to the riches of his glory, he may grant that you may be strengthened in your inner being with power through his Spirit, and that Christ may dwell in your hearts through faith, as you are being rooted and grounded in love. I pray that you may have the power to comprehend, with all the saints, what is the breadth and length and height and depth, and to know the love of Christ that surpasses knowledge, so that you may be filled with all the fullness of God.

1. Recall a childhood memory with a friend. What is something about yourself you remember in that friendship that is sometimes lost or blurred today?
2. Name a hope you have for your child or children as they make friends. Share that hope with your kids either by telling them or writing it to them in a note.
3. Do you feel content with your friends in this season of life? Do they help you to feel heard and loved, just as you are? To whom do you offer that kind of friendship?
4. What adult friendships did you see when you were growing up? How are your friendships today the same or different from the adult friendships you witnessed growing up?

CHAPTER 6

Rest

"In our own contemporary context of the rat race of anxiety, the celebration of Sabbath is an act of both resistance and alternative. It is resistance because it is a visible insistence that our lives are not defined by the production and consumption of commodity goods."

~ *Walter Brueggemann*[19]

For the first half of my career as a pastor, an underlying theme haunted my days: "Try harder." My misconception led me to push past the deep rest needed to do the deep, thought-filled work. I watched the clock to count that I worked enough hours to count as a real pastor. I was available every second of each day for pastoral care for all ages. I presumed if I kept trying harder and clocked longer hours, sacrificed more, and grew adequately tired, I was doing good work.

Brueggemann's rat race of productivity in my work included these endless tasks: Interpret the Scriptures and the budget, listen to people and pray with them, answer the phone at all hours of the day and night, drive away from my house to the familiar scene of a toddler banging in protest at the window as he watched his mom's car disappear down the street.

There have been seasons in my career that have been propelled by the need to prove I was a pastor doing good work. I showed up even when I did not need to. I worried about people's perception

---

[19] Walter Brueggemann, *Sabbath as Resistance: Saying No To a Culture of Now* (Louisville: Westminster, 2017) (revised), p. xiv.

of me when it was unnecessary. I look back in regret at the number of bath times and bedtimes, date nights, and family time I missed, mistakenly setting my family in second place.

I now know that in the trying harder I neglected my own human need for reflection and rest.

Human Bodies Are Designed to Need Rest

Human bodies dearly need regular rest. No one would argue with such indisputable logic. Bodies which soak up more sleep are more efficient leaders, exercise better judgement, and tend to be more pleasant. Good sleepers often live longer.

The vocation of pastor is not naturally a restful one. Consequently, it is not unusual for pastors to struggle with depression and weight gain. My denomination's benefits program annually invents creative ways to change the curve (so to say). Clergy are famous for an inadequate amount of rest.

And then there are parents, most of whom are not pastors. The parenting journey begins with rest-deprivation.

Parents do not wake up in the morning with fully rested bodies; they awake when another body needs something, usually food or cuddling. A parent's need for rest is surrendered, night after night, month after month, year after year after year.

"They never want to go to bed...Every morning when I wake up, my first thought is, 'When can I come back here?' It's the carrot that keeps me motivated... Ironically, to my children, bedtime is a punishment that violates their basic rights as human beings. Once the lights are out, you can expect at least an hour of inmates clanging their tin cups on the cell bars."

~ *Jim Gaffigan*[20]

People assure me that not long after kids are old enough to sleep through the night, they are old enough to go out at night with friends. Again, sleep is lost. Later, kids move out of the house and begin their parent-free lives, doing who knows what who knows where. Who can sleep? In the midst of that insomnia, families like ours joyfully add a puppy to the family and on the nights all the kids are actually sleeping peacefully, the dog walks figure-eights on the end of the bed all night, like Gideon sounding the trumpet for sleep deprivation to continue its invasion. Oh sleep, where art thou? Why hast thou vanished forever?

Before we give up on healthy rest, as though it is a lost dream that did not come true, remember God's ancient innovation called Sabbath. Along the West Coast, there is a group of people whose practice of Sabbath gives me hope that rest is actually possible.

How Sabbath Began

In Loma Linda, California, people are living up to 10 years longer than the average American[21]. This Southern California community

---

[20] Jim Gaffigan, *Dad is Fat* (New York: Three Rivers Press, 2013), p. 186.
[21] Dan Buettner. https://www.bluezones.com/exploration/loma-linda-california. 2008.

is called a Blue Zone®, identified by Dan Buettner as one of five areas in the world where people live the longest and healthiest.

Much of the population of Loma Linda belongs to a Christian denomination called Seventh Day Adventist. From sundown on Friday to sundown on Saturday, Adventists faithfully practice Sabbath rest. They spend the 24 hours of Sabbath with family, worshiping and eating with their community of faith, and playing and walking out in nature. Their intentional sabbath time, they believe, relieves stress, encourages exercise, and strengthens their relationships with family and church community.

Imagine some of what the Adventists in Loma Linda are *not* doing for an entire 24 hours. They are not going to work, scrolling absent-mindedly through Instagram, shopping Amazon's latest deals, paying bills, attending grandkids' sporting events, or going to the grocery store. They are not doing the things that typically fill up our day without our even noticing.

Sabbath is more than going to church or keeping stores closed on Sundays. Sabbath is a practice God gave to us in order to keep humans human.

It went like this. When the Israelites were wandering through the wilderness, God summoned their wilderness guide, Moses, to the top of Mount Sinai to issue a few rules. (Ten rules, to be precise.) The Israelites needed rules to create order in their lives and in their nomadic community. Wandering was hard enough without understanding it was wrong to yearn for your neighbor's wife and cow.

God began the list of rules by reminding them what they already knew. There was only one God, and it was none of them. Only God was God, able to transform into a cloud, a fire, or a person as needed. With that rule established, God kindly asked them to speak the name of God nicely.

The next rule is the longest of all ten. Before God issued any rules about how to treat one another, God introduced the notion of Sabbath, like a beautifully wrapped gift.

> Remember the sabbath day and keep it holy. Six days you shall labor and do all your work. But the seventh day is a sabbath to the Lord your God; you shall not do any work – you, your son or your daughter, your male or female slave (21st century reader, don't get hung up there), your livestock, or the alien resident in your towns. For in six days the Lord made heaven and earth, the sea, and all that is in them, but rested the seventh day; therefore the Lord blessed the sabbath day and consecrated it. (Exodus 20:8-11)

In no uncertain terms, God explained that if God could take an entire day to rest from making the *universe*, a human being can rest, too. We can rest from the many tasks we devote ourselves to throughout the day. Tasks like doing the dishes, grocery shopping, yardwork, paying the bills are necessary tasks. I feel like a taskmaster wizard on days I make my to-do list and victoriously check off each item.

Sabbath is the opposite of being productive. It is counter to anything that involves consuming or producing. Why would God speak at length of Sabbath? Because already, only a few years into their wandering in the wilderness, the Israelites had forgotten how they got there.

How Quickly We Forget

The entire Jewish faith and then Christian faith depended on each generation telling the history of faith practices to the next generation. Let's imagine one day in the desert, an Israelite grandma took her young granddaughter for a walk. The granddaughter was chilly and did not own a scarf, so she asked her grandma if they might trade some of their flour for material to make a scarf.

"Not today," grandma gently explained, "today is the sabbath."

"I already took a bath yesterday. And what is sab," granddaughter whined.

"No," said grandma, covering up her giggle. "Sabbath is a gift God gave us. We are not to make trades or do any kind of work on this day."

"Seems like a waste," countered the wise and candid young girl.

"Maybe so. Let me tell you a story," began the grandma. "Not so long ago, my parents grew up in Egypt, a country filled with glamorous pyramids, built like triangles so high their tips tickled the clouds."

The granddaughter looked up, imagining a triangle climbing high into the sky.

"It sounds beautiful, but the pyramids were built by my grandparents and the family members of all the people walking with us through this wilderness. They worked day and night, even when they were sick, even when their backs felt like breaking, even when all they wanted to do was sleep."

"Why did they do that?" the granddaughter asked, fearful this might be her future, too.

"They worked so hard building the pyramids because Pharaoh demanded it. He was the boss, and not a kind one. The work grew so tiresome, never ending day after day, that our people cried to God. And God listened. God heard the cries of our people and had a long talk with Pharaoh. You will understand the story as you get older. God made a way for my grandparents and everyone else to leave their brick-making jobs and find a new home. That is why we are walking, my granddaughter. God is leading us to a new home where there are no bricks to build day after day. Our backs are not breaking and our work will not be so hard."

"And that is why there is a sabbath day?"

"Yes, God gave us the gift of a sabbath day. A day to rest and be free from our work, so that we do not forget what our families endured in Egypt. We rest because human bodies are not made to work as Pharaoh ordered. We are made to work, and also to rest. So, your scarf will wait until tomorrow. For today, my sweater will keep you warm."

Practicing Sabbath

For practicing Jews, the duration of the Sabbath, known as Shabbot, is stunning. For Orthodox Jews, all work ceases and life pauses in a unique way. There is no electricity, no transportation, no cooking. For Christians, Sabbath is treated differently. Even if a person who is Christian has a day off from paid work on a Sunday, it is unlikely that Christian will do no other productive work on the Sabbath, (unless that Christian resides in Loma Linda, California).

True Sabbath means no lawn work or laundry. No grocery shopping or fixing the leaky faucet. True Sabbath also means no shopping. It is, calling to mind the wisdom of Walter Brueggemann, halting the cycle of our contemporary brickmaking. Our bodies are not built for work day in and day out, nor are they meant to mindlessly consume. We are limited, mortal bodies who, long ago, received the gift of freedom from work for one day out of seven.

Lauren Winner, author and lecturer, was raised Jewish and now serves as an Episcopal priest. She writes of integrating her Jewish

Shabbot (Sabbath) practices into her Christian practices in her thoughtful book, *Mudhouse Sabbath*[22].

> "But there is something in the Jewish Sabbath that is absent from Christian Sundays: a true cessation from the rhythms of work and world, a wholy set apart, and perhaps, above all, a sense that the point of Shabbot, the orientation of Shabbot, is toward God." Lauren Winner, Mudhouse Sabbath, Chapter 1

Sabbath is less about what we cease to do and more about ceasing our confusion about God's gift of our own bodies. Our bodies belong to God, not to the productivity of the world. My body does not belong to the endless work of pastoral care, or doing dishes, laundry, or refereeing my three favorite kids in the universe. Sabbath is not about "completing tasks," but recognizing my "completeness" as child of God through the mercy of God in Jesus Christ.

What Might Sabbath Really Look Like?

One of the sages of our time, Pastor Eugene Peterson, wrote about Sabbath in his last of many books, *Pastor: A Memoir*[23]. Throughout his life as a pastor, he and his wife very intentionally set aside Mondays not as a day off, but as Sabbath.

> We quit taking a "day off" and began keeping a "Sabbath," a day in which we deliberately separated ourselves from the work week - in our case being pastor and pastor's wife - and gave ourselves to being present to what God has

---

[22] Lauren Winner, *Mudhouse Sabbath: An Invitation to a Life of Spiritual Discipline* (Lauren Winner, 2003), p. 10.
[23] Eugene Peterson, *Pastor: A Memoir* (New York: HarperCollins, 2011), p. 220.

done and is doing, this creation in which we have been set down and this salvation in which we have been invited to be participants in a God-revealed life of resurrection.

I, too, set Mondays aside as my Sabbath. It is a day to leisurely read and write. A day to slow down, take my dog on walks, and sit still. However, I am no Sabbath purist. While Pastor Peterson could define the boundaries of his Sabbath faithfully and in an inspiring way, I find that to be impossible. There is constantly a list in front of me reminding me to meal plan, budget, pay bills, run errands, and respond to the latest need in my family. I feel excited about tackling that list on Mondays.

And that is just fine. My Sabbath need not look exactly like Eugene Peterson's or yours. My Sabbath includes breaks from screens, permission to be more than a productive person, a nap, and hopefully coffee with a dear friend. It is a tremendous challenge for me, but I hope to teach my kids that our value is not dependent upon making bricks, getting work done, or accomplishing as much as possible each and every day.

In March 2020, the entire world took on a Sabbath pace. Of course, for people who worked in essential fields, life sped up instead of slowed down. But we all quickly adjusted to a new pace because there was no other choice. In my own home, we no longer hustled to get ready for work and school in the morning. The family calendar went blank. I bought one tank of gas for an entire month, instead of a week.

For many weeks, much of what we had planned for our lives simply did not happen. Although there was devastation to be felt by many through those weeks, it is fascinating that much of what we did not do simply went undone.

Our family rested in abundance, played more games, grew exhausted of one another other's company, and had to come to terms with managing a freer schedule. It was uneasy to suddenly live with a freer schedule in place of one that was tightly knit together, with one full day unfolding into the next.

Sabbath for Women

How often have you heard or responded to the question, "How are you?" with the word, "Busy"? This is not consistent among cultures, but it is particularly true in the United States, where worth is often defined by a person's hyper-instrumentalization and not by our wisdom about rest. Often, the more visible a person's hard work, the more they are compensated. White bodies more than black bodies, and male bodies more than female bodies.

Through the years, I have visited with a plethora of women who simply assume they should be busy. If a task might be easy, we tend to make it harder. For example, who invented ironing? Good grief, that was an unnecessary move, and I think I hate you, whoever you are, inventor of ironing.

When we assign chores among family members, women typically assign the majority of chores to themselves, with a proclivity to assume the administrative chores, known as the mental load. While the guys might go out to socialize at the end of the work week, women come directly home to make supper. Men have hobbies, like participating in outdoor sports or religiously following a sports team. A woman's hobbies are often packed away while she is raising kids. Only when she is an empty nester, cleaning out her kid's old room will she discover the box containing a time capsule of hobbies she enjoyed before having kids.

"At a certain age almost all the questions a person asks him or herself are really about one thing: how should you live your life?"

~ *Britt-Marie*[24]

A woman once shared with her friends that her husband was training for a marathon. Hours and hours each week he dedicated to this challenging goal, lacing up his running shoes and jogging out the door. While she felt proud of his ambition and commitment, she admitted to her friends, "I wish I had hours and hours to run."

Ours is not a culture that teaches women the importance of Sabbath. Instead, we grow tired and then bitter, resentful when we set aside our own interests and hobbies in order to administer the traditional production of home and family.

Even the Body of God Needed to Rest

In fact, our ancestors were freed from the sort of nonsense that discourages a person from resting. In the Gospels, Jesus disappeared from time to time for Sabbath moments. He is in the thick of the crowd and then suddenly he is nowhere to be found. The deep rest of Sabbath prepared him for the deep work of healing and teaching.

It was Jesus' practice to step back from the wildness of life and the demands around him to rest. He deliberately left the scene in order to pray and restore his God-given humanity. He could have been healing people, preaching, or teaching, but instead, he was sitting

---

[24] Fredrik Backman, *Britt-Marie Was Here* (New York: Simon & Schuster, 2014), p. 261.

there. "Don't just do something, sit there," I once heard in a sermon. Our model for such wisdom is none other than the only human who literally could do it all. But instead of doing, Jesus was sitting.

The Sabbath, however it might look in your life, with or without enough sleep, is a gift from God to you. It is a sort of reminder that your body may not have come with an instruction manual, but if it did, to rest might be the most important instruction of all.

Read of the disciples' productive work in Mark 6:30-32. Jesus responds with a simple instruction.

30The apostles gathered around Jesus, and told him all that they had done and taught. 31He said to them, "Come away to a deserted place all by yourselves and rest a while." For many were coming and going, and they had no leisure even to eat. 32And they went away in the boat to a deserted place by themselves.

1. If you had an entire day to yourself, how might you spend it?
2. What expectations keep you from setting aside time for yourself? Where did those expectations come from?
3. What did you learn from the pandemic in 2020 about slowing down?

CHAPTER 7

Rituals

"Lord,

it is night.

The night is for stillness.

Let us be still in the presence of God."[25]

~ *A Night Prayer from the New Zealand Prayer Book*

New Parent Revelation #14: Putting a child to bed demands the imagination of J.K. Rowling and the stamina of Richard Simmons.

Back when I knew everything about being a parent, that is, before I became one, I surmised putting a child to bed is a task that happens every single night so really, who cares? How hard can it be? Bath, pajamas, tuck in, voila. See you in the morning!

I could not have been more wrong. To any parent with whom I ever underestimated the demanding work of putting a child to bed, I am so very sorry.

The ritual of putting a child to bed night after night (and then not resting, as you read in chapter six) can be like running a marathon when you only trained for a 5K. I cannot put into words how exhausting, how depleting, how humbling bedtime can be. There is no promise of the beloved night prayer's stillness in the first hour

---

[25] *A New Zealand Prayer Book, He Karakia Mihinare, o Aotearoa.* (New Zealand: Anglican Church, 1989), p. 184.

or more of the adventure.

Teaching the Ritual of Practicing the Christian Faith

When our first child was born, I was serving as the associate pastor at Holy Nativity Lutheran Church in New Hope, Minnesota, a suburb tucked into the edge of the west side of Minneapolis. My work included nurturing faith in children, youth, and families.

Lutheran churches often turn to programs like Sunday School and Confirmation to nurture faith in children and youth. But these programs tend to be feeble attempts in classrooms to pour knowledge into kids' brains more than nurture their faith in Jesus Christ. I understand this as a parent. I drop off my kids at a variety of places in hopes of giving them a well-rounded life experience. Piling into the car most days, I drop them off to practice piano, football, basketball, marimba, baseball, softball, gymnastics, or dance. It seems obvious that I would also drop them off at church to give them a little practice being a Christian. I understand why parents like me might expect their child to have a relationship with Jesus by taking them to the place where we talk about him the most.

However, faith, much like algebra, is not absorbed by osmosis. We do not *learn* rituals of the Christian faith in the same way we learn a basketball drill or a marimba piece. I am afraid children and youth learn much less than we would like to admit in programs like Sunday School and Confirmation. In fact, pastors like me might cry our eyes out if we had our own come-to-Jesus moments with these two ministries. Jesus may be a bit heartbroken to know he had to die so teenagers could suffer through memorizing what Martin Luther had to say about sex.

Faith is not something we learn in a classroom.

When Classroom Learning Was Not the Right Answer

In the introduction to a famous parable called "The Parable of the Good Samaritan," a Confirmation alumni posed a question for Jesus. The story is told only in the Gospel of Luke, the writer who cared deeply for the people most forgotten, including the poor and the broken. Unlike the Gospel of Matthew, which affirms the importance of learning the right stuff in a Confirmation classroom, Luke is more about what difference all those lessons might make for the marginalized people with whom Jesus hung out.

"Teacher," asked someone who wanted to see if Jesus learned as much in Confirmation as he had, "what must I do to inherit eternal life?"

How I do wish the Bible was originally written as a digitized, multi-dimensional book with layers of information. I would love to touch this story and hear the tone of Jesus' voice. Was he sarcastic with this Confirmation goody-goody? Did his face reveal annoyance or sheer delight at the open lay-up to slam dunk the ridiculous worship of religious knowledge? But alas, because the Bible is written only one-dimensionally, I am going to imagine the latter.

Jesus replied, "What is written in the law? What do you read there?"

"You shall love the Lord your God with all your soul, and with all your strength, and with all your mind; and your neighbor as yourself." And Jesus said to him, "You have given the right answer; do this, and you will live." Jesus went on to tell a subversive story of radical, counter-cultural love for the very people whom the person who asked the question probably despised.

Sure, the Confirmation star gave the right answer because he knew the right stuff, but now he had to *do* the stuff! The only way we can do the very hard stuff of loving God and loving our neighbor requires us not to be in a classroom, but out in the world with people.

At the time I attended seminary, students spent one of our four years on internship. I struck a gold mine at my internship church, where I was surrounded by an encouraging congregation and brilliant pastors.

I learned from the two wise pastors at Oak Grove Lutheran, south of Minneapolis, that faith is about relationships, not programs. Pastor Tom Zarth and Pastor Brice Eichlersmith, (whom I mentioned in chapter five) modeled nurturing faith by sitting with people. The rituals they practiced included prayer and asking critical questions to help people grow deeper into their Christian faith. I spent a year with two pastors who loved teaching Confirmation because they were teaching students about relationships, much to the chagrin of the Confirmation star in Luke's Gospel.

Later, in my first call, I was curious about how nurturing faith could be more centered in relationships than programs. I attended a presentation at Luther Seminary by Marilyn Sharpe, who was part of the Youth and Family Institute® at the time. Actually, I waddled into the presentation, pregnant enough to attract the unsolicited advice of the women in the room who had a knack for unsolicited advice.

Marilyn presented on the importance of rituals. A ritual is something practiced regularly that provides constancy. Whereas our daily lives are often frantic and frenetic, a ritual smooths out our lives.

A ritual could be a daily walk, prayer, or cup of coffee. It could be an annual vacation, cheering on a favorite sports team faithfully each week, or celebrating birthdays. Rituals come in all shapes and sizes. They are not necessarily related to practicing a faith. The purpose of a ritual is to insert a framework where life is constantly pushing at the edges.

One of the rituals Dr. Sharpe suggested all those years ago has stuck. It has been a part of our family ever since that day I sat uncomfortably at a table with a dozen people yearning to help people slow down and breathe in the incredible gift of faith and make sense of life.

> "I love ritual and repetition. Without them, I would be a balloon with a slow leak."
>
> ~ *Anne Lamott*[26]

Marilyn offered an example of a simple bedtime ritual and for me, it stuck. For most of their lives, I have practiced the ritual of making the sign of the cross on my kids' foreheads, tracing the watery symbol that first marked them in their baptisms.

The Ritual of Holy Baptism

There is no standard way to explain the ritual of Holy Baptism across all Christian denominations. In the denomination I serve, the Evangelical Lutheran Church in America (ELCA), Baptism is not a prevention program to escape a bad afterlife. It is not about saving a person from the fiery streets of hell. Baptism has less to do with heaven and hell and more to do with God's unconditional promise to shape our everyday lives on earth.

It is a beautiful moment when a person is baptized and a watery cross is traced on a person's forehead. The watery cross is a symbol

---

[26] Anne Lamott, *Stitches: A Handbook on Meaning, Hope, and Repair*, (New York: Riverhead Press, 2013), p. 82.

of the promise that baptism claims us as God's own beloved forever and ever. In the ELCA, the majority of the newly baptized are infants. They are no less able to fathom the mystery of God's mercy than anyone else in the room of any generation. As that child grows in years, the promise of God's irreversible mercy will sometimes feel uncertain or even futile. The watery cross will be forgotten.

Age can threaten to snag the fearfully wonderful weaving of the Maker. As the years add up, so might our skepticism. An unconditional promise in a culture built upon the conditional "if-then" becomes suspicious. In Kindergarten, the child who was given an unconditional baptismal promise will also hear, "If you behave, then you are awarded a star at the end of the day." A few years later, the condition might be, "If you earn good grades, then you deserve a scholarship." Or, "If you follow that group, then you will be accepted." After graduation, the message evolves to, "If you work hard, then you are paid." And, "If you sacrifice, then you succeed."

There is no age group easier to teach about God's unconditional promise and irrevocable grace than children. They simply understand in the purest of ways that God loves them no matter what, without condition. For that reason, I did my best in their early bedtime days to remind my kids.

A Sticky Ritual Even (and especially) with Teenagers

Beginning in the hospital on their first day outside the womb, long before a baptism, and later on in what I hoped was the final tuck-in at night, but almost never was, I traced the tiny cross on their tiny foreheads and whispered, "Jesus loves you." It was our sticky ritual.

"Jesus loves you," I continued to remind my wiggly toddlers. Often, they would remind me of God's clingy grace, too, so I shut my eyes lest a wayward little finger poke it out as it traced the cross on my own forehead and my child whispered to me, "Jesus loves you."

"Jesus loves you," I remind my teenager not every single night but whenever I suspect I'm allowed to be affectionate. Rituals get trickier as children get older, let me tell you. Rituals with littles who think their parents are da bomb? Piece of cake. Rituals with big kids who can't believe God stuck them with these parents and these siblings? No cake there.

Teenagers are not the only ones who learn to be tricky as they add numbers to their age; so do their moms. When I'm near enough to my teenagers at worship during the Confession and Absolution, I try my darndest to trace that cross on their foreheads. They need to remember God's unconditional promise as teenagers more than ever.

"Perhaps home is not a place but simply an irrevocable condition."

~ *James Baldwin*[27]

Conditions are the steepest and ugliest for teenagers. "If you like my post, then I'll like yours." "If you hate him, then I will hate him, too." "If you ignore her, then we can be besties." "If you give up that value of yours, then we can have more fun." "If you risk your parents' trust, then your tribe of friends will admire you."

Long before I became a mom of teenagers, I was getting ready. A pastor has the privilege of working with every generation of families, including emerging young adults. Most pastors teach

---

[27] James Baldwin, *Giovanni's Room*, (New York: Vintage Books, 2013), p. 92.

teenagers, preach to them, and hang out with them.

I am constantly learning from teenagers who live with one foot in a world in which they know they are loved and belong, and another foot in a world in which belonging is an endless test of "if-then" conditions. Through sermons, classes, and conversations I have tried to tell teenagers and kids preparing for teenage-dom how much God loves them and will never stop.

When I teach parents about baptism, I ask them to practice the nightly, sticky ritual of making the sign of the cross on their child's forehead because the older a child gets, the more ridiculous the stories become about what it takes to be loved and to belong.

I knew this was coming when my oldest started school. It became a ritual on the eve of the first day of school to read Max Lucado's profound children's book, *You Are Special*[28]. I could preach a thousand sermons about love and belonging, but this book would outshine any of them. We read this book about the Wemmicks giving stars and dots to the cool and the uncool, and we talked about what kinds of stars and dots would be given in Kindergarten. And then in First Grade. And then in Second Grade. And later in Middle School.

Although this book is a beautiful children's book, it is a sneaky teenager book, too. It sneaks in the message that stars and dots are made up. No one gets to tell someone else whether they matter and whether they belong.

The kinds of jeans they wear and the number or letter behind their iPhone do not get to claim how much they matter. How many friends and what they dare post on Snapchat don't determine it, either. They are so loved, I remind them, because the promise of God's sticky grace is plastered on their foreheads in the shape of an indelible cross and that claim can never be erased. As their friends

---

[28] Max Lucado, *You Are Special*, (Wheaton: Crossway Books, 1997).

come and go and they make mistakes big and small, God will love them no matter what. In case they don't listen to me, which happens with teenagers and their mothers, I say it again and again, sometimes with words, sometimes with hugs, and other times with donuts.

The cross on their foreheads contradicts much of what they are told about the world and their place in it. It is possible they might listen to me and believe they are loved simply because God created them to love them.

I've noticed when my sons tuck in their little sister, a rare but touching occasion, they might trace the cross on her forehead. And sometimes, albeit rarely, she even does it back.

Reading Rituals

That's the thing about rituals, they tend to stick. Do something night after night and your child might do it, too. But before we made it to the conclusion of the bedtime routine with the reminder "Jesus Loves You" and the last kiss and hug, however, books were in order.

The OB-GYN who checked on my first son and me in the hospital the day after he was born preached a pithy sermon about reading to my son. "Read him anything. Any words you can find, read them to him. Read him a book, read him the newspaper. Just read!"

And so, I read.

I was stocked with books because the generous women at the first church I served made sure I was. At what was, in my estimation, the most beautiful baby shower ever thrown in the history of babies, they filled our bookshelves with *Good Night Moon*, *Harold and Purple Crayon*, and everything Eric Carle had ever written. I laughed with my kiddos over *Parts* and accompanied Max where *The Wild Things Are*. In one of the dozen baby Bibles we were given, we told our son the stories of God's unrelenting love, even when we wander like the Prodigal Son, disobey like King David, and simply can't believe it, like most of the disciples.

Reading books is a sticky ritual that marks the end of the day even though a single day with a child writes enough tales for a book of its own.

And finally, when the bedtime rituals are complete, there is stillness. Standing outside the door, every time you put a child to bed is a mind-blowing moment. "I put a child to bed!" I would celebrate, in my head mimicking Tom Hanks in "Castaway"[29] when he started a fire and beat his chest. "I [chest beating] have put a child to bed!" The stillness never stops producing amazement.

When children outgrow their original bedtime routines, other rituals shape the night. Tucking in teenagers at my house means asking questions. "When are you going to bed?" "Where exactly are all your devices which should not go to bed in the same room as you." And finally, "I'm going to bed. Do the right thing and just don't be dumb."

In the end, we depend on sticky rituals to root children in the few things that really do matter in our families. Sometimes kids will get it right, and other times, well, there are new mercies to be found in a new day.

---

[29] *Castaway*. Directed by Robert Zemeckis, DreamWorks Pictures, 2000.

Read Isaiah 58:11, an example of the Lord's ritual work in you, and how life-giving rituals are meant to be.

"The Lord will guide you continually, and satisfy your needs in parched places, and make your bones strong, and you shall be like a watered garden, like a spring of water, whose waters never fail."

1. What children's books do you remember reading as a child or reading to a child?
2. What ritual do you remember as a child? How did your family celebrate birthdays or practice faith or eat meals?
3. What are rituals you currently practicing individually or with family to give order to the day and night?

Made in the USA
Middletown, DE
26 September 2021